Strimko Book 1

150 Easy-to-Master Number Logic Puzzles

Serhiy Grabarchuk
Tanya Grabarchuk
Peter Grabarchuk
Helen Grabarchuk

 Puzzlium, Inc.
San Diego, California

Content

Introduction

Strimko™ is a logic number puzzle invented by The Grabarchuk Family in 2008. It is based on the idea of Latin squares described by a Swiss mathematician and physicist Leonhard Euler (1707-1783) in the 18th century.

All Strimko puzzles are solvable with a pure logic, no special knowledge is required. Strimko uses only three basic elements: rows, columns, and streams. All elements have equal numbers of cells, and the goal is to make each row, column, and stream containing the whole set of specified numbers. Cells in the grid are organized into several streams of equal length, which often run diagonally and even branching. Such mechanics creates entangled patterns resulting in interesting challenges and unusual logic.

This book contains a specially designed collection of 150 easy-to-master puzzles with 4 x 4 through 7 x 7 grid sizes. Puzzles are arranged from the easiest to the hardest ones so that you'll progress in solving skills with each next puzzle.

Strimko challenges were handcrafted by Helen, Tanya, Serhiy, and Peter Grabarchuk, and up to date hundreds of original Strimko puzzles were published in various forms and platforms. Learn more at strimko.com.

Happy puzzling!   – Serhiy and Peter Grabarchuk
                                    San Diego, CA, USA

v1.3.5

Rules

The object of the puzzle is to fully fill in the given grid with missing numbers observing three simple rules. You have numbers 1 through 4 for a 4 x 4 grid, 1 through 5 for a 5 x 5 grid, 1 through 6 for a 6 x 6 grid, and 1 through 7 for a 7 x 7 grid.

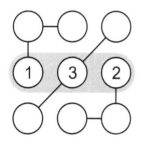

Rule #1
Each row must contain different numbers.

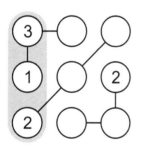

Rule #2
Each column must contain different numbers.

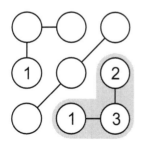

Rule #3
Each stream must contain different numbers.

Solver's Guide

Here are basic methods that may be used to solve Strimko.

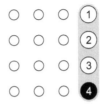

Method 1
Determine a row's last missing number.

Method 2
Determine a column's last missing number.

Method 3
Determine a stream's last missing number.

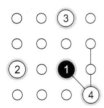

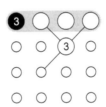

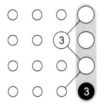

Method 4
Determine a number in an intersection (row/column/stream) whose cells already contain all but one value.

Method 5
Determine a number in a row, if all of its free cells but one are eliminated by a number from outside the row.

Method 6
Determine a number in a column, if all of its free cells but one are eliminated by a number from outside the column.

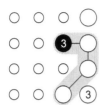 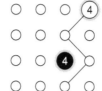 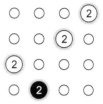

Method 7
Determine a number in a stream, if all of its free cells but one are eliminated by a number from outside the stream.

Method 8
Determine a number, if its cell eliminates all cells in another stream but one which already has a number.

Method 9
Determine a number, if all other numbers of the same value are already presented in the grid.

Example

Here is how a simple 3 x 3 Strimko logic puzzle can be solved in four steps.

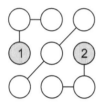

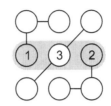

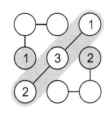

Start

Let's solve the easiest 3 x 3 Strimko logic puzzle step-by-step.

Step 1

In the second row only one number is missing. Thus we can put in the grid our first number, 3.

Step 2

In the diagonal stream we can put in its top right cell only 1, and in its bottom left cell only 2. One stream is fully filled now.

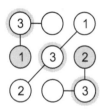

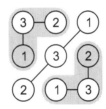

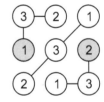

Step 3

Now we can put two missing 3's; they must go in the middle cells of the two opposite corner-like streams.

Step 4

Finally, we have to complete both corner-like streams putting 2 in the top vacant cell, and 1 in the bottom one.

Finish

Congratulations! You have solved your first Strimko logic puzzle.

Grabarchuk

Puzzles

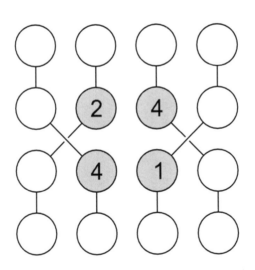

1

2

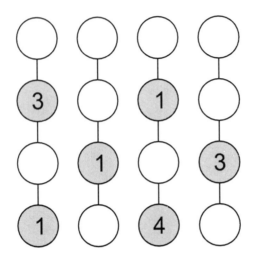

Grabarchuk

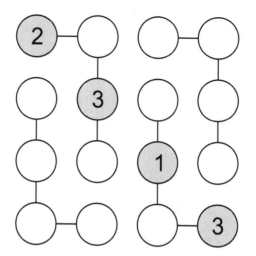

3

4

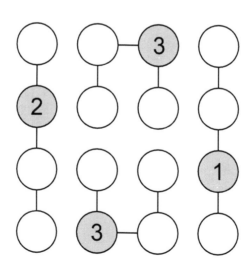

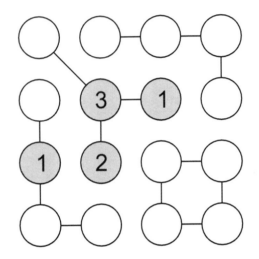

5

6

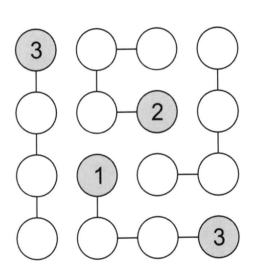

Grabarchuk

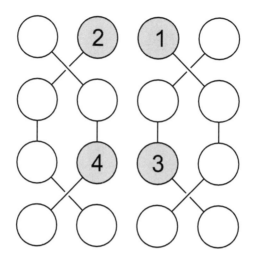

7

8

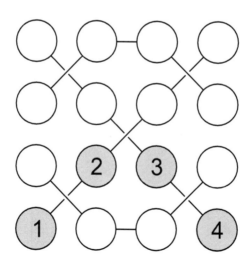

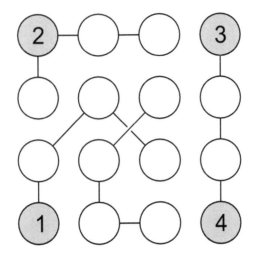

9

Grabarchuk

11

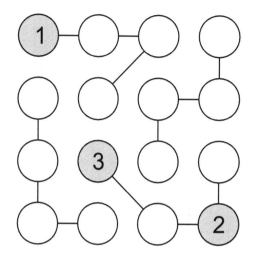

12

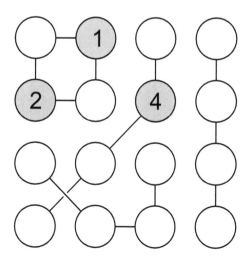

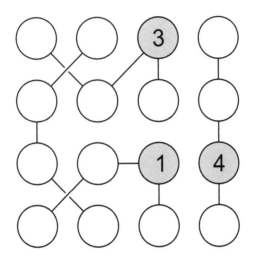

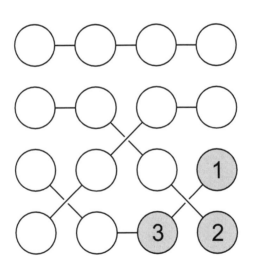

Grabarchuk

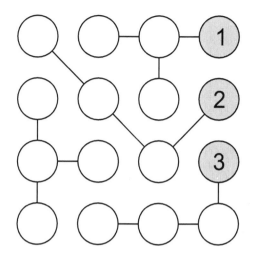

15

16

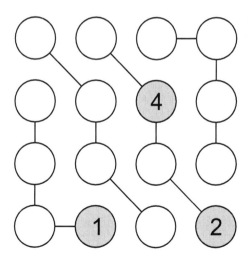

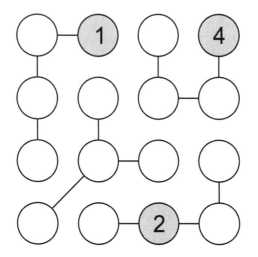

17

18

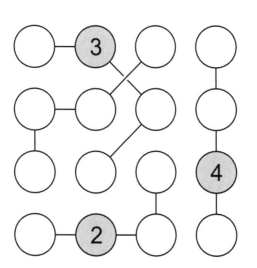

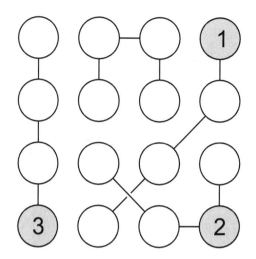

19

20

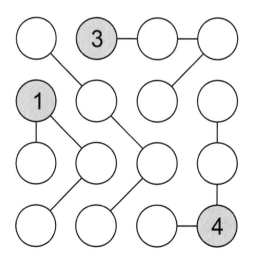

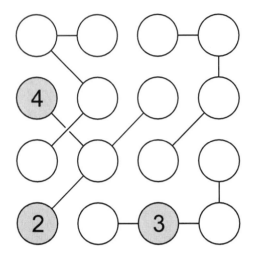

21

22

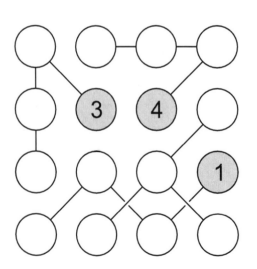

Grabarchuk

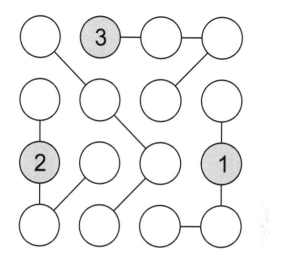

23

24

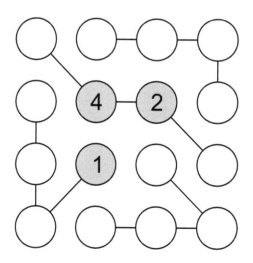

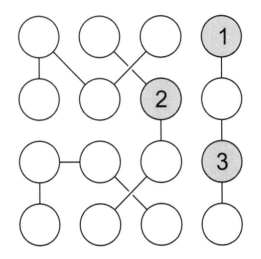

25

26

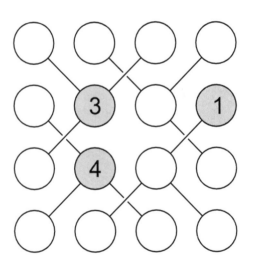

Grabarchuk

27

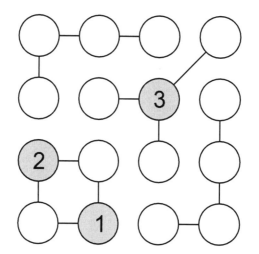

28

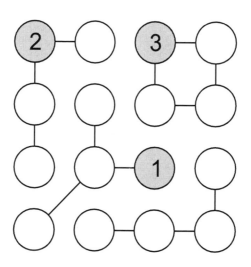

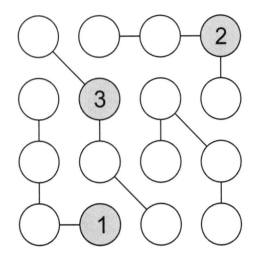

29

30

Grabarchuk

31

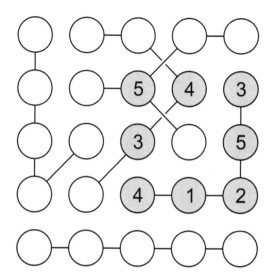

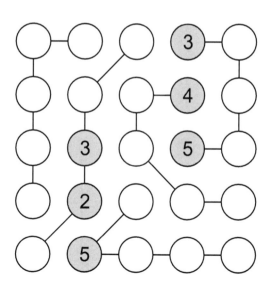

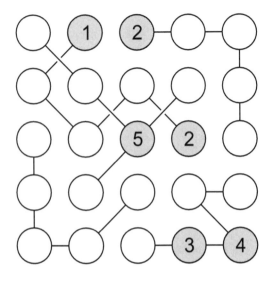

33

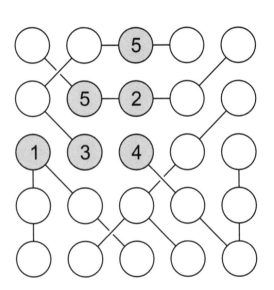

34

Grabarchuk

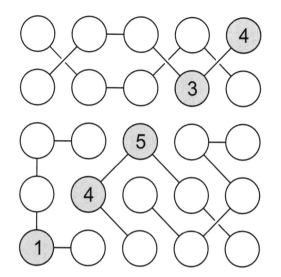

35

36

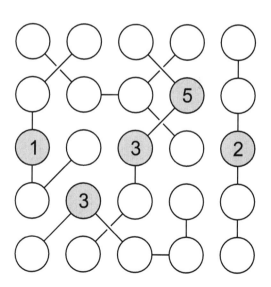

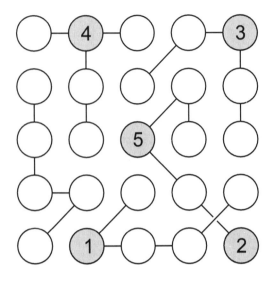

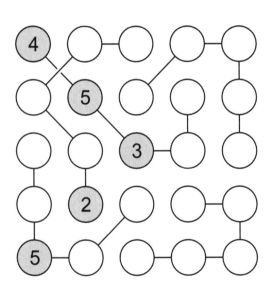

Grabarchuk

39

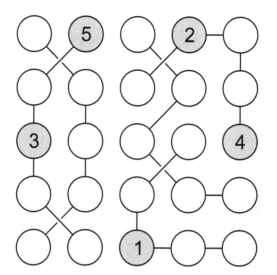

40

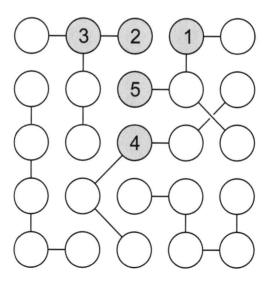

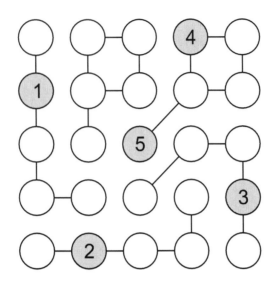

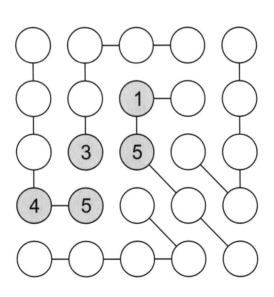

Grabarchuk

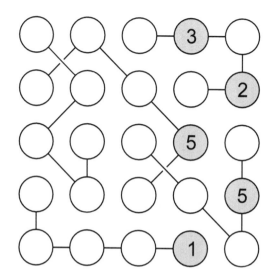

43

44

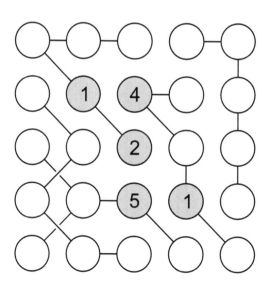

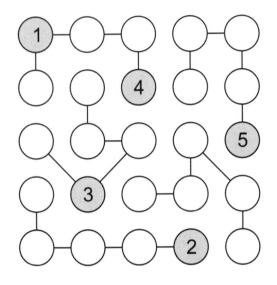

45

46

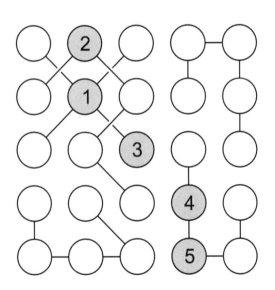

47

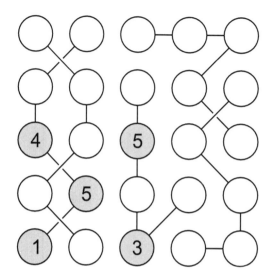

48

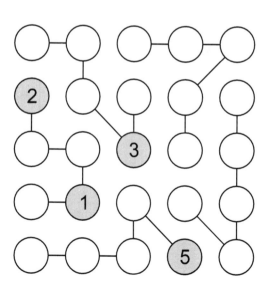

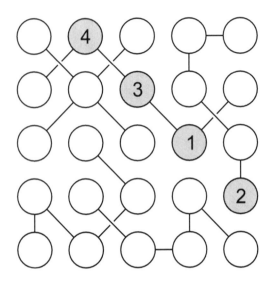

49

50

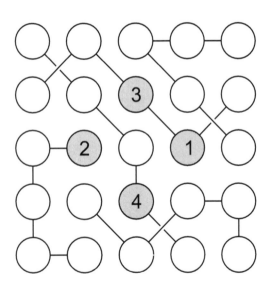

Grabarchuk

51

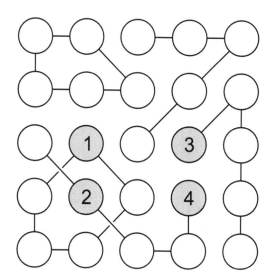

52

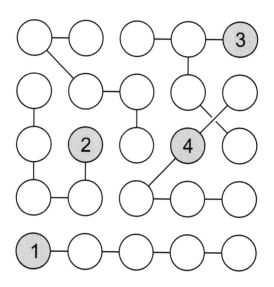

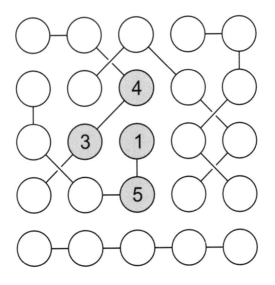

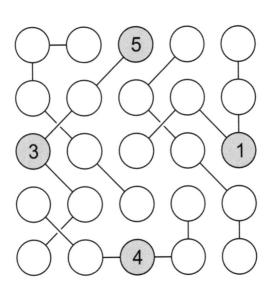

Grabarchuk

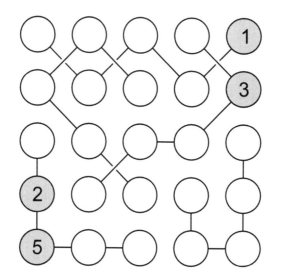

55

56

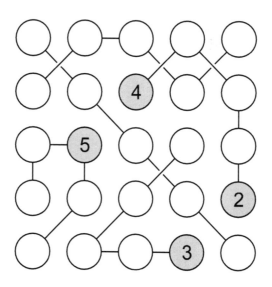

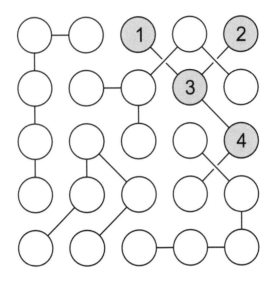

57

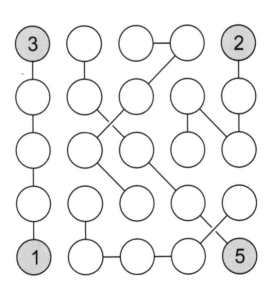

Grabarchuk

59

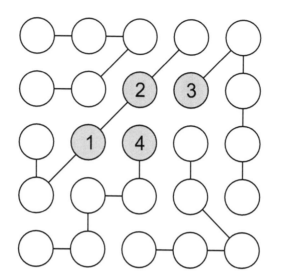

60

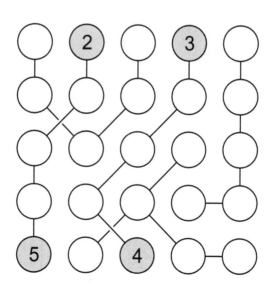

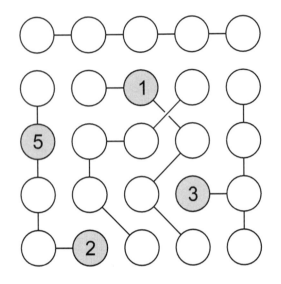

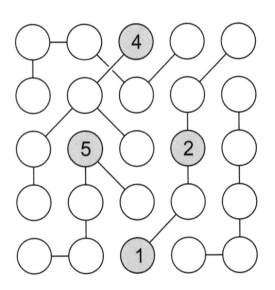

Grabarchuk

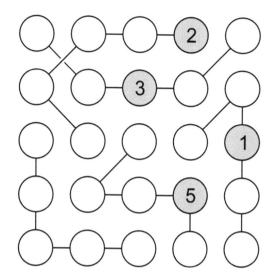

63

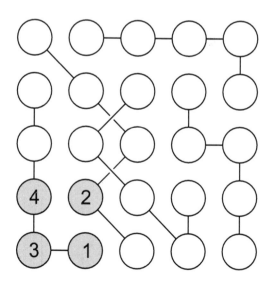

64

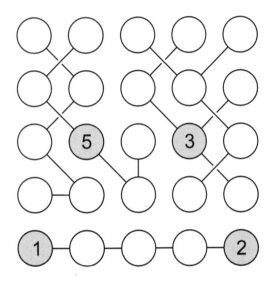

65

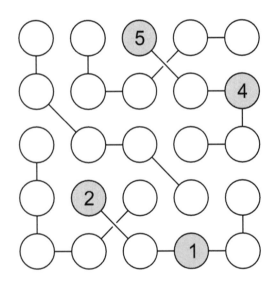

66

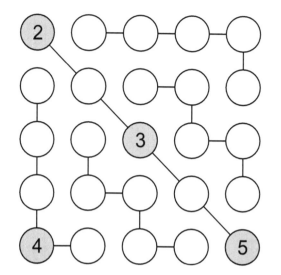

67

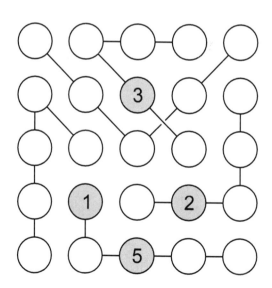

68

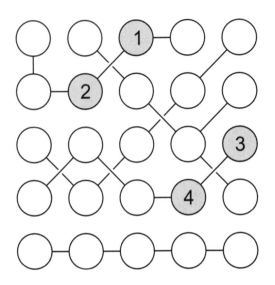

69

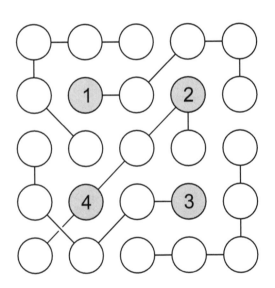

70

Grabarchuk

71

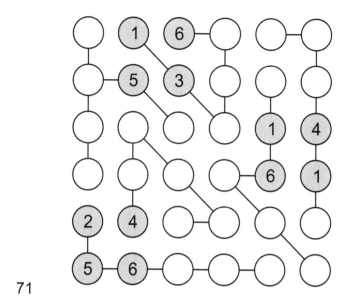

72

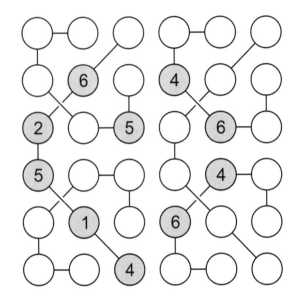

73

74

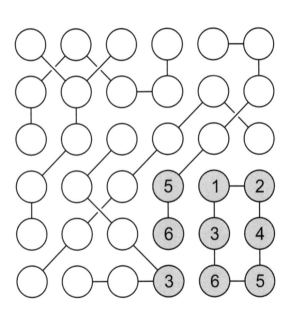

Grabarchuk

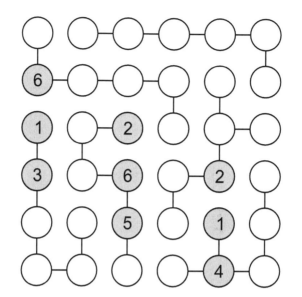

75

76

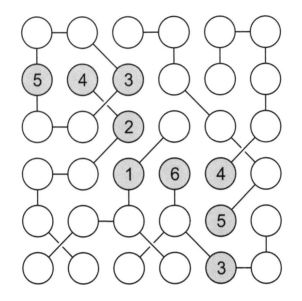

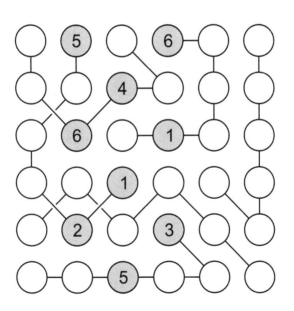

Grabarchuk

79

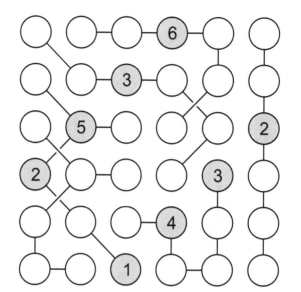

80

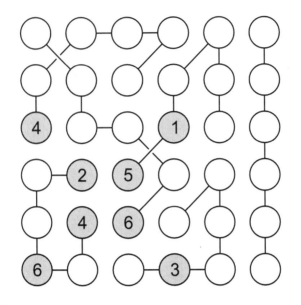

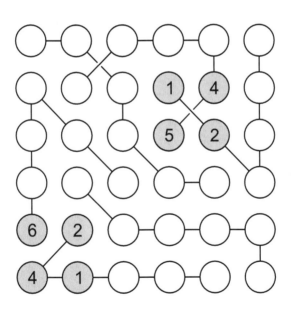

Grabarchuk

83

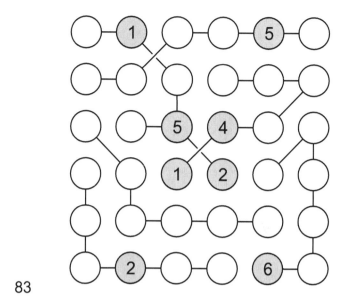

84

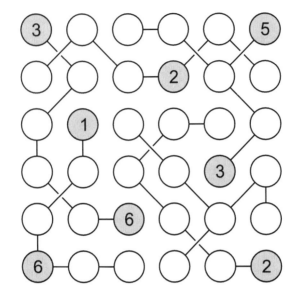

85

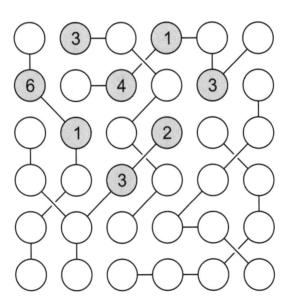

Grabarchuk

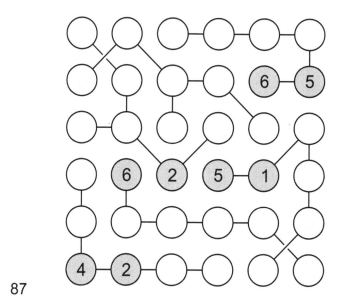

87

88

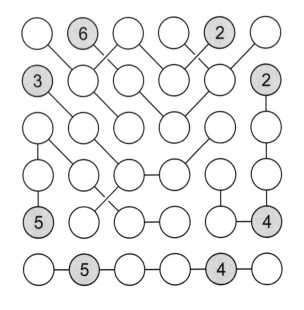

89

90

Grabarchuk

91

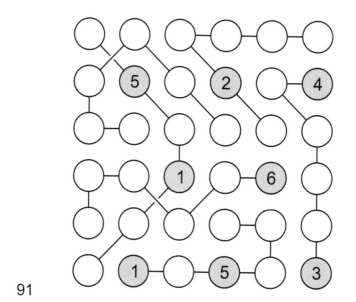

92

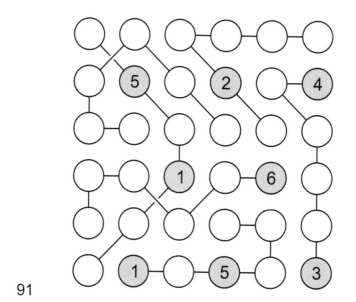

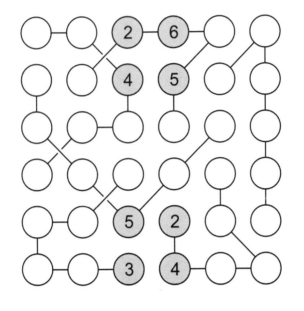

93

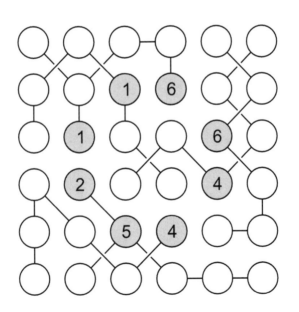

Grabarchuk

95

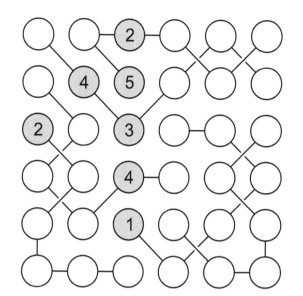

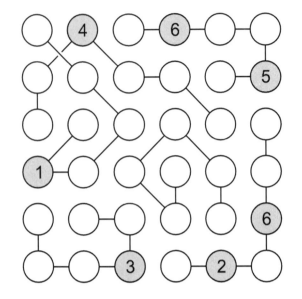

97

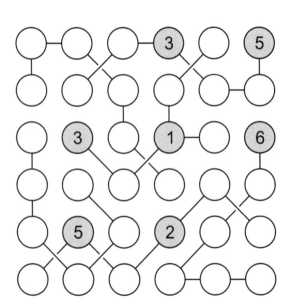

Grabarchuk

99

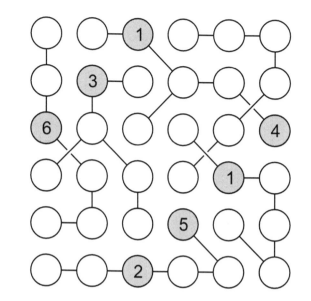

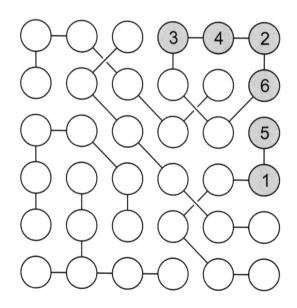

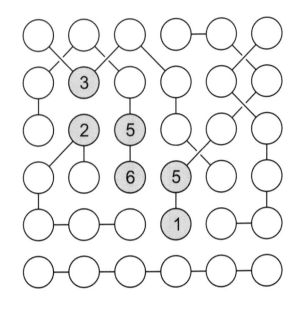

101

102

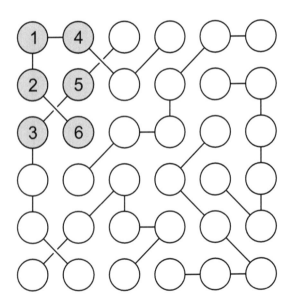

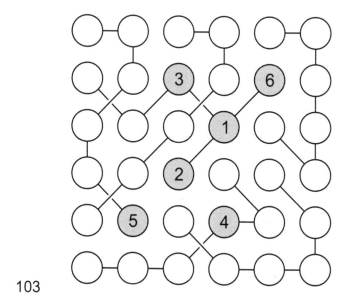

103

104

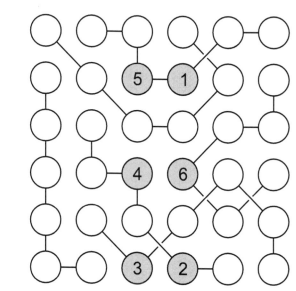

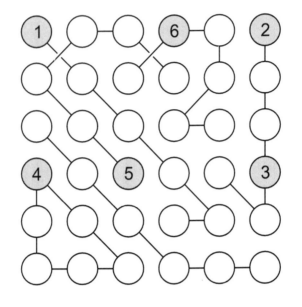

105

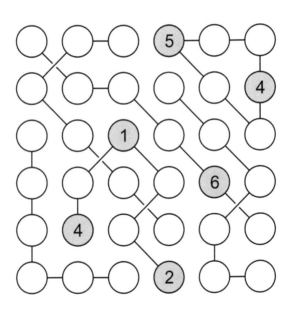

Grabarchuk

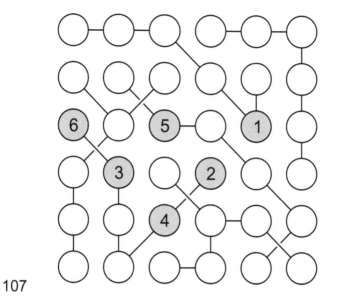

107

108

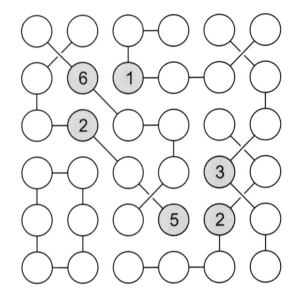

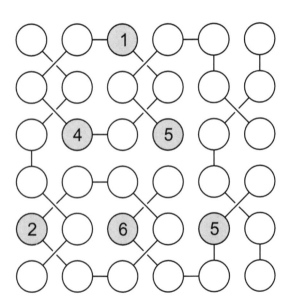

Grabarchuk

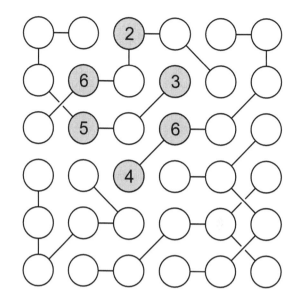

111

112

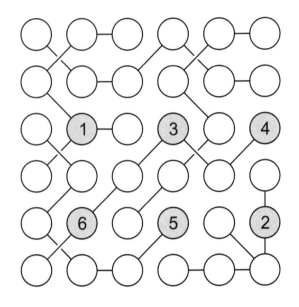

113

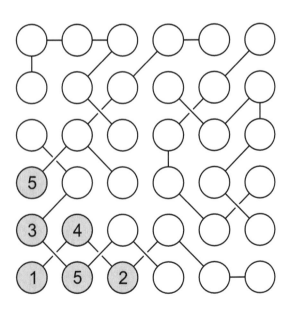

Grabarchuk

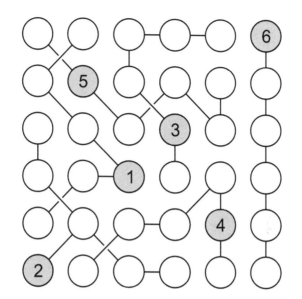

115

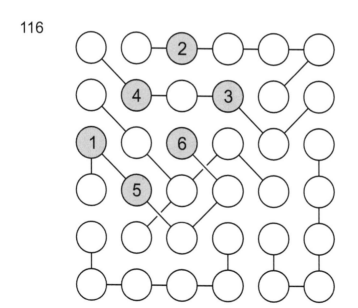

116

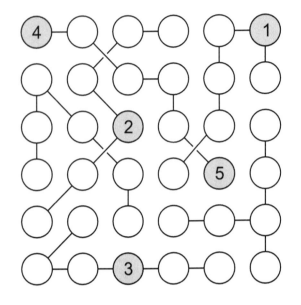

117

118

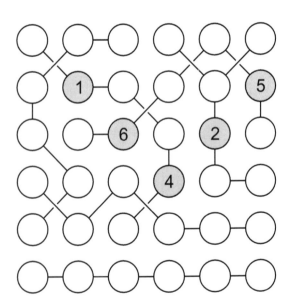

Grabarchuk

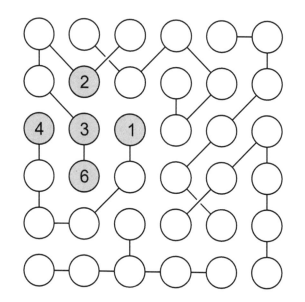

119

120

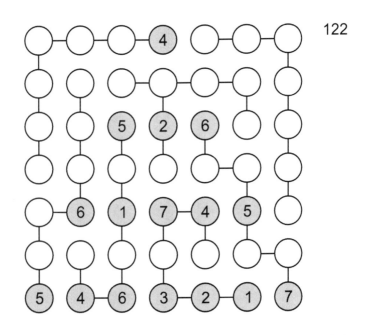

121

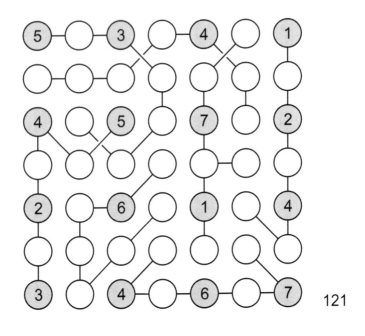

122

Grabarchuk

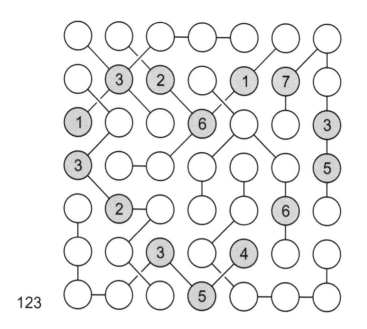

123

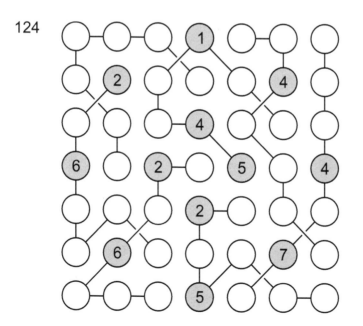

124

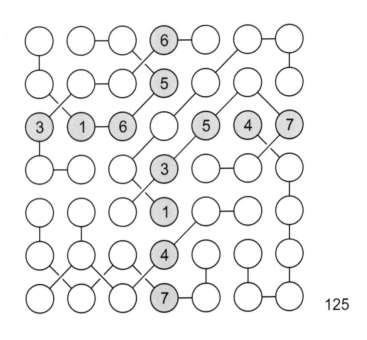

125

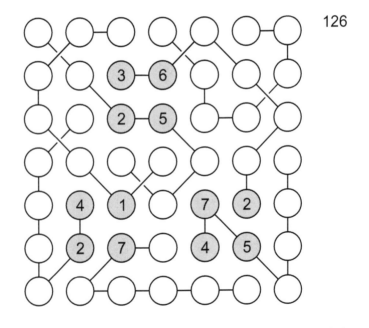

126

Grabarchuk

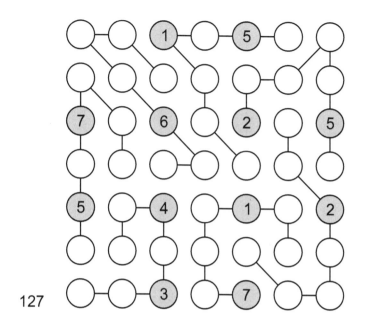

127

128

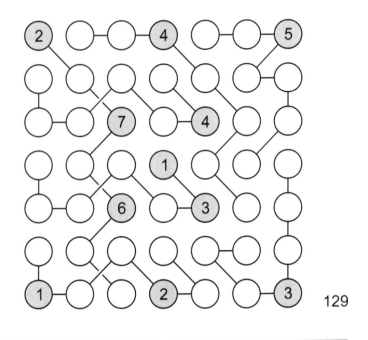

129

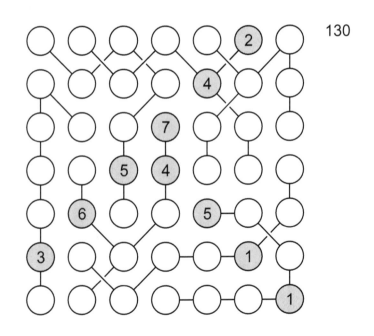

130

Grabarchuk

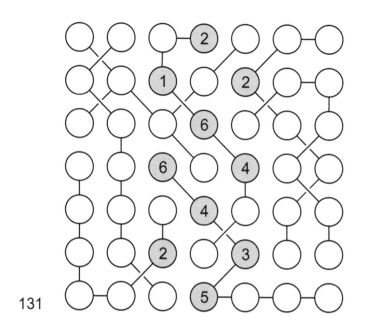

131

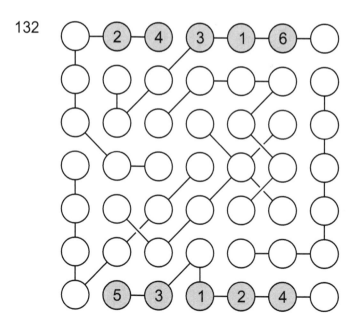

132

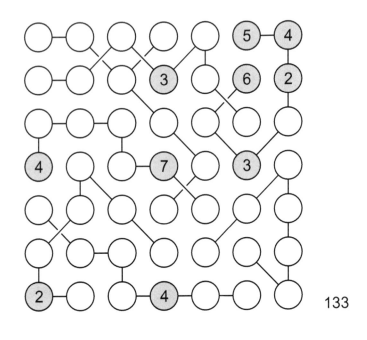

133

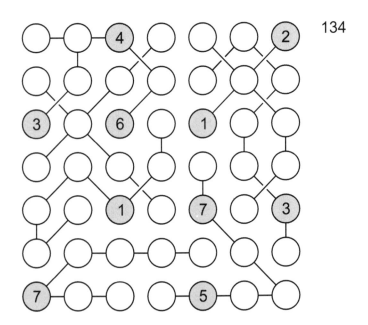

134

Grabarchuk

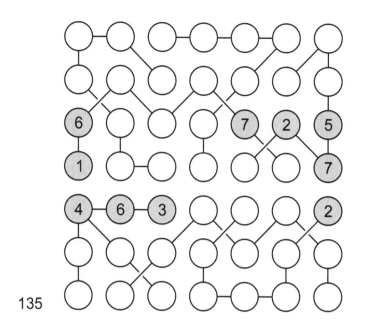

135

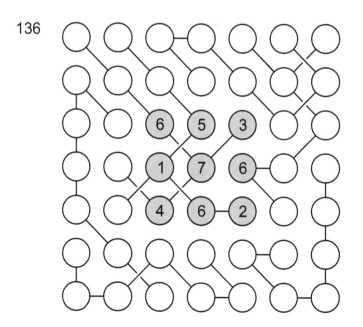

136

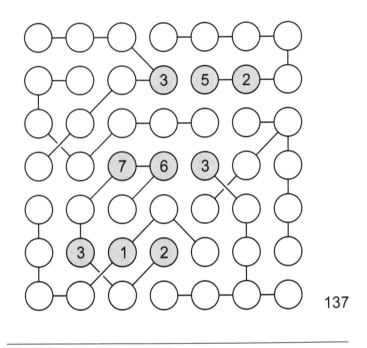

137

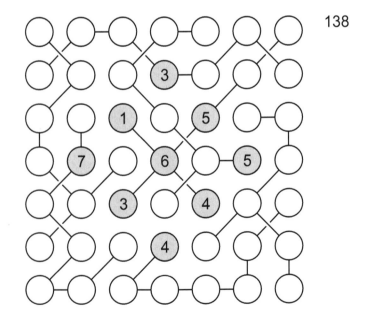

Grabarchuk

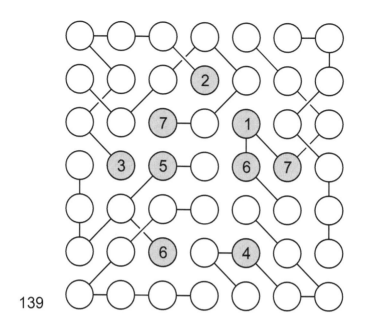

139

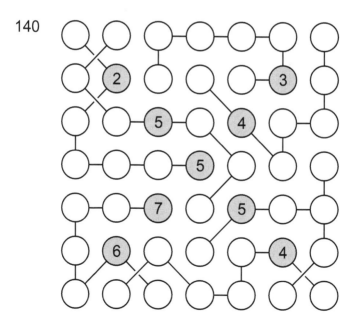

140

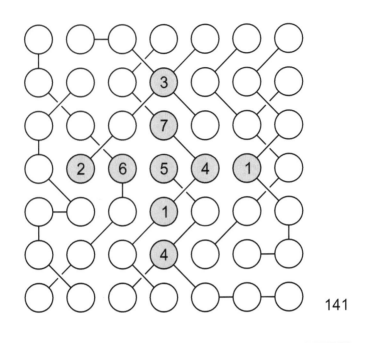

141

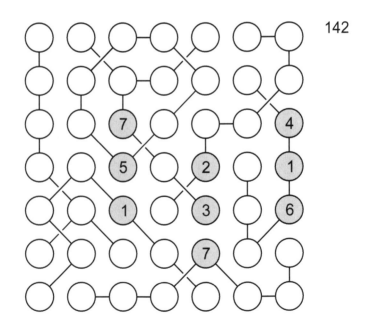

142

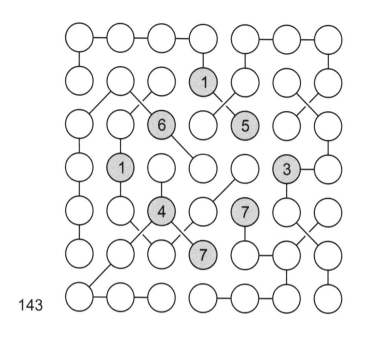

143

144

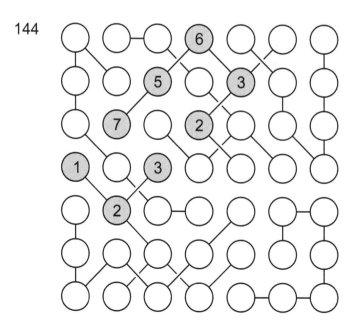

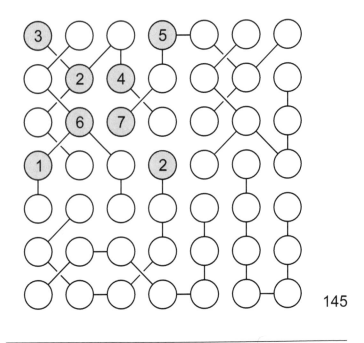

145

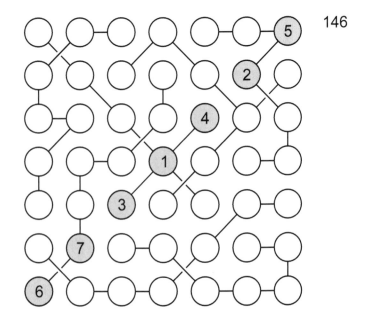

146

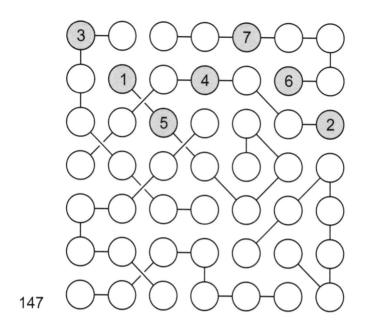

147

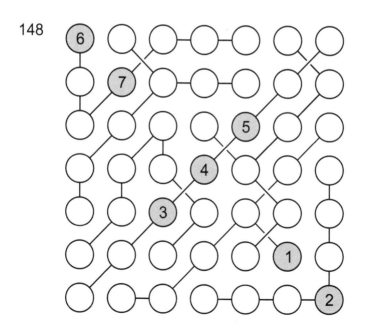

148

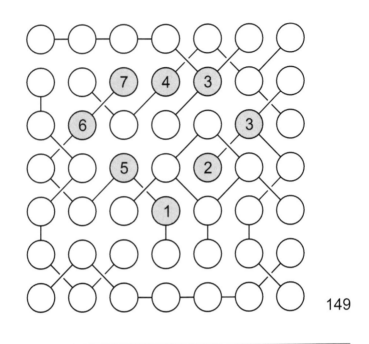

149

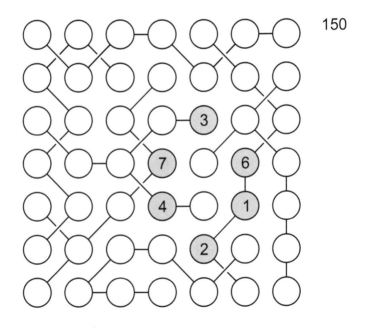

150

Grabarchuk

Solutions

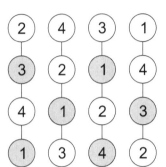

1

2

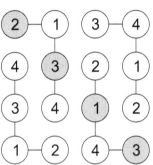

3

4

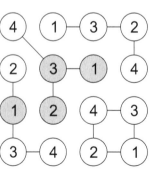

5

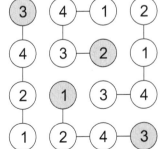

6

Grabarchuk

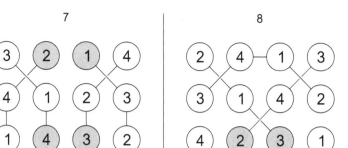

7

3 2 1 4
4 1 2 3
1 4 3 2
2 3 4 1

8

2 4 1 3
3 1 4 2
4 2 3 1
1 3 2 4

9

2 4 1 3
3 2 4 1
4 1 3 2
1 3 2 4

10

1 3 2 4
3 2 4 1
4 1 3 2
2 4 1 3

11

1 2 3 4
2 4 1 3
4 3 2 1
3 1 4 2

12

4 1 3 2
2 3 4 1
3 2 1 4
1 4 2 3

13

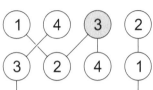

14

15

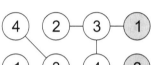

16

17

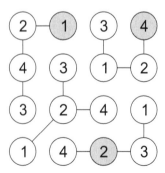

18

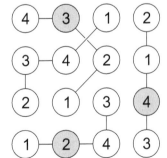

Grabarchuk

19

4	2 — 3	1	
2	1	4	3
1	3	2	4
3	4	1	2

20

4	3 — 1	2	
1	2	4	3
2	4	3	1
3	1	2 — 4	

21

3 — 4	2 — 1		
4	2	1	3
1	3	4	2
2	1	3 — 4	

22

4	2 — 1	3	
1	3	4	2
2	4	3	1
3	1	2	4

23

4	3 — 1	2	
1	2	4	3
2	4	3	1
3	1	2	4

24

1	2 — 3	4	
3	4 — 2	1	
2	1	4	3
4	3 — 1	2	

25

2	3	4	1
3	1	2	4
4	2	1	3
1	4	3	2

26

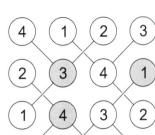

27

1	3	2	4
4	2	3	1
2	4	1	3
3	1	4	2

28

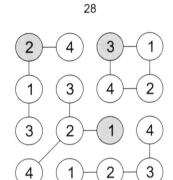

29

1	4	3	2
4	3	2	1
3	2	1	4
2	1	4	3

30

3	2	1	4
4	3	2	1
2	1	4	3
1	4	3	2

Grabarchuk

31

```
5 — 2 — 1 — 3 — 4
2 — 1 — 5 — 4 — 3
1 — 4 — 3 — 2 — 5
3 — 5 — 4 — 1 — 2
4 — 3 — 2 — 5 — 1
```

32

```
2 — 4 — 5 — 3 — 1
5 — 1 — 3 — 4 — 2
1 — 3 — 2 — 5 — 4
3 — 2 — 4 — 1 — 5
4 — 5 — 1 — 2 — 3
```

33

```
3 — 1 — 2 — 4 — 5
5 — 2 — 4 — 1 — 3
4 — 3 — 5 — 2 — 1
1 — 4 — 3 — 5 — 2
2 — 5 — 1 — 3 — 4
```

34

```
3 — 1 — 5 — 2 — 4
4 — 5 — 2 — 1 — 3
1 — 3 — 4 — 5 — 2
2 — 4 — 1 — 3 — 5
5 — 2 — 3 — 4 — 1
```

35

```
3 — 2 — 1 — 5 — 4
5 — 1 — 4 — 3 — 2
4 — 3 — 5 — 2 — 1
2 — 4 — 3 — 1 — 5
1 — 5 — 2 — 4 — 3
```

36

```
5 — 4 — 2 — 3 — 1
3 — 2 — 1 — 5 — 4
1 — 5 — 3 — 4 — 2
2 — 3 — 4 — 1 — 5
4 — 1 — 5 — 2 — 3
```

37

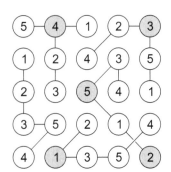

38

39

40

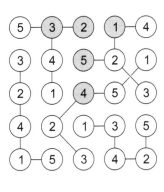

41

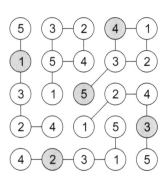

42

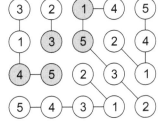

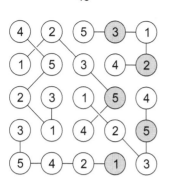

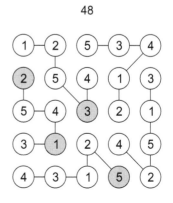

49

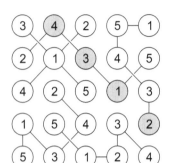

50

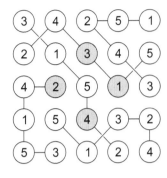

51

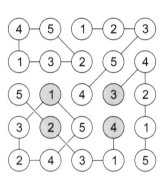

52

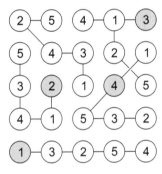

53

54

Grabarchuk

55

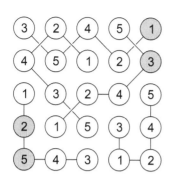

56

57

58

59

60

61

62

63

64

65

66

94

Grabarchuk

67

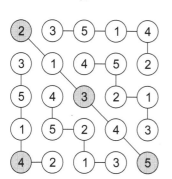

68

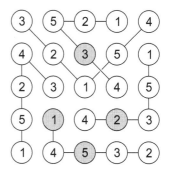

69

```
3 — 4 — 1 — 5 — 2
4 — 2 — 3 — 1 — 5
5 — 1 — 4 — 2 — 3
2 — 3 — 5 — 4 — 1
1 — 5 — 2 — 3 — 4
```

70

```
1 — 3 — 4 — 5 — 2
5 — 1 — 3 — 2 — 4
4 — 2 — 5 — 1 — 3
2 — 4 — 1 — 3 — 5
3 — 5 — 2 — 4 — 1
```

71

```
3 — 1 — 6 — 4 — 2 — 5
1 — 5 — 3 — 2 — 4 — 6
6 — 3 — 2 — 5 — 1 — 4
4 — 2 — 5 — 3 — 6 — 1
2 — 4 — 1 — 6 — 5 — 3
5 — 6 — 4 — 1 — 3 — 2
```

72

```
6 — 1 — 5 — 4 — 2 — 3
1 — 6 — 3 — 2 — 4 — 5
2 — 5 — 4 — 3 — 1 — 6
4 — 3 — 2 — 5 — 6 — 1
3 — 4 — 1 — 6 — 5 — 2
5 — 2 — 6 — 1 — 3 — 4
```

73

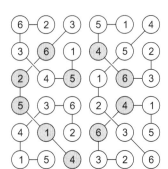

74

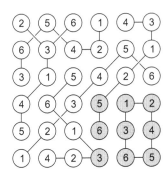

75

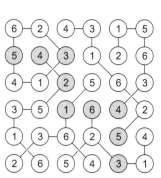

76

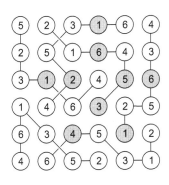

77

78

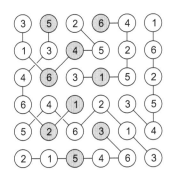

79

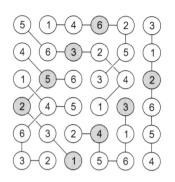

80

81

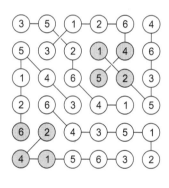

82

83

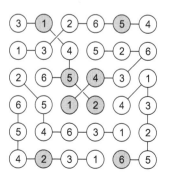

84

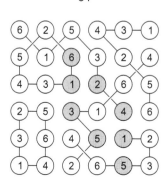

85

3	6	2	1	4	5
5	4	1	2	6	3
2	1	3	6	5	4
1	2	4	5	3	6
4	5	6	3	2	1
6	3	5	4	1	2

86

4	3	2	1	6	5
6	2	4	5	3	1
5	1	6	2	4	3
1	5	3	4	2	6
3	4	1	6	5	2
2	6	5	3	1	4

87

6	5	1	4	2	3
2	4	3	1	6	5
5	1	6	3	4	2
3	6	2	5	1	4
1	3	4	2	5	6
4	2	5	6	3	1

88

6	1	4	2	3	5
3	5	1	4	2	6
4	2	5	3	6	1
2	4	6	1	5	3
5	3	2	6	1	4
1	6	3	5	4	2

89

1	6	5	4	2	3
3	4	1	6	5	2
4	1	3	2	6	5
2	3	4	5	1	6
5	2	6	1	3	4
6	5	2	3	4	1

90

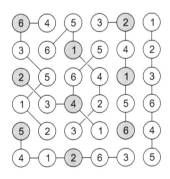

6	4	5	3	2	1
3	6	1	5	4	2
2	5	6	4	1	3
1	3	4	2	5	6
5	2	3	1	6	4
4	1	2	6	3	5

Grabarchuk

91

92

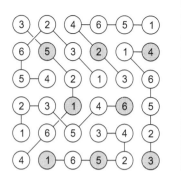

93

94

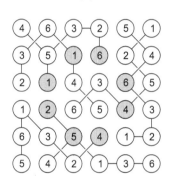

95

96

97

98

99

100

101

102

Grabarchuk

103

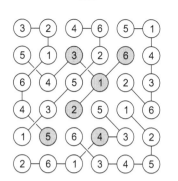

104

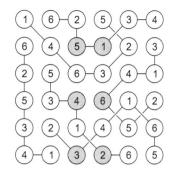

105

106

107

108

109

110

111

112

113

114

Grabarchuk

115

4	3	2	5	1	6
6	5	4	1	3	2
1	4	6	3	2	5
3	2	1	6	5	4
5	6	3	2	4	1
2	1	5	4	6	3

116

6	1	2	4	5	3
2	4	5	3	6	1
1	3	6	5	2	4
3	5	1	2	4	6
5	6	4	1	3	2
4	2	3	6	1	5

117

4	2	5	6	3	1
2	1	6	3	4	5
5	3	2	1	6	4
6	4	1	2	5	3
3	6	4	5	1	2
1	5	3	4	2	6

118

6	2	5	1	3	4
4	1	3	2	6	5
3	4	6	5	2	1
2	6	1	4	5	3
1	5	2	3	4	6
5	3	4	6	1	2

119

5	1	4	2	6	3
1	2	6	4	3	5
4	3	1	5	2	6
2	6	3	1	5	4
6	5	2	3	4	1
3	4	5	6	1	2

120

2	4	6	5	1	3
3	1	5	6	4	2
1	5	4	3	2	6
6	3	1	2	5	4
5	6	2	4	3	1
4	2	3	1	6	5

121

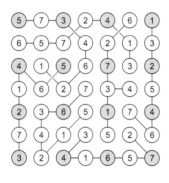

122

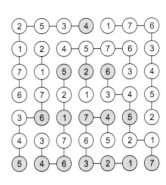

123

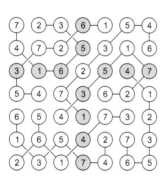

124

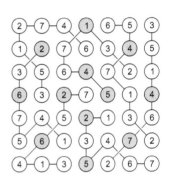

125

126

Grabarchuk

127

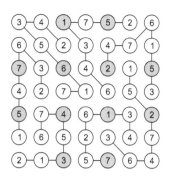

128

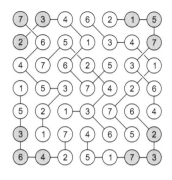

129

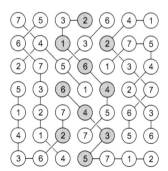

130

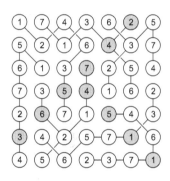

131

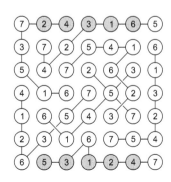

132

133　　　　134

135　　　　136

137　　　　138

Grabarchuk

139

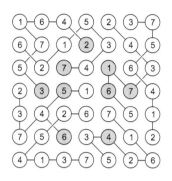

140

141

142

143

144

145

146

147

148

149

150

Grabarchuk

Made in the USA
Lexington, KY
23 November 2017